"Faithful, theologically rich children's books are a rare treat in
Christian publishing. Laferton has provided us with one of the best little
treatments of biblical theology available for parents to read to their children. *The
Garden, the Curtain and the Cross* not only teaches children stories in the Bible but
the story of the Bible—one that culminates in the atoning work of Jesus Christ who
gives broken sinners access to God. This book is a tremendous resource for parents
and children who want to better understand the grand storyline of Scripture."

R. ALBERT MOHLER, JR, President of the
Southern Baptist Theological Seminary

"I am so excited about this book! It is colorful, engaging,
and creative, and that's just the icing on the cake! *The Garden, the Curtain
and the Cross* is a brilliant re-telling of the one story that rules all other
stories. I cannot commend this book highly enough. Read it to your children,
give it to your neighbors, and talk about what it means to live in light of
the fact that the curtain has been torn."

GLORIA FURMAN, Cross-cultural worker, author of
The Pastor's Wife and *Missional Motherhood*

thegoodbook
for children

The Garden, the Curtain and the Cross
© Catalina Echeverri / The Good Book Company 2016.
Reprinted 2016 (three times), 2017 (twice), 2018 (three times), 2019.

"The Good Book For Children" is an imprint of The Good Book Company Ltd.
Tel: 0333 123 0880 International: +44 (0) 208 942 0880   Email: info@thegoodbook.co.uk

UK: www.thegoodbook.co.uk North America: www.thegoodbook.com
Australia: www.thegoodbook.com.au New Zealand: www.thegoodbook.co.nz

Illustrated by Catalina Echeverri | Art Direction & Design by André Parker

ISBN: 9781784980122 | Printed in India

THE GARDEN

THE CURTAIN

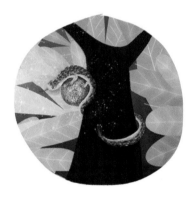

AND THE CROSS

WRITTEN BY:
CARL LAFERTON

ILLUSTRATED BY:
CATALINA ECHEVERRI

A very long time ago, right here in this world,

there was a garden.

In the garden,
everything was wonderful.
The world was full of laughing
and playing and smiling and fun.

There was nothing bad, ever.
There was no one sad, ever.
And best of all...

GOD
was there!

HELLO
ADAM
hello Eve

He had **MADE** it all.
He was in **CHARGE**
of it all.
He **LOVED** it all.

People could see God,
and speak to God,
and just enjoy *being*
with God.

It was wonderful
to live with God.
But then, one day...

The people did a
terrible thing.

They decided they
didn't want to do
what God said.

They decided they
wanted a world
without God in charge.

God calls this "sin".
Sin spoils things. So sin has no place in God's wonderful garden.
God said to the people,
"You can't live with me in my garden anymore..."
And he sent them outside.

To show the people they had to stay outside,
God put some warrior angels in front of the garden.
The angels were like a big KEEP OUT sign.

Now things were sometimes bad,
and people were sometimes sad.

But people STILL kept sinning because
they didn't want God to be in charge.

So no one could come into
God's wonderful place.

God said, *Because of your sin,*
you can't come in.

God wanted people to remember:
It is wonderful to live with him...
but because of your sin, you can't come in.

So he told the people to build a special building
called his temple, where he would live.

In the middle of the temple was the most
wonderful place in the world - the place where
God was, with nothing bad and nothing sad.

It was VERY exciting...

But then God told people to put
A BIG CURTAIN around this
wonderful place.
The curtain had pictures of
warrior angels on it.
It was a big KEEP OUT sign.

For hundreds of years, the temple
curtain reminded people that God said,

It is wonderful to live with him,
but because of your sin,
you can't come in.

Babies became grown-ups
and had babies...
and those babies became
grown-ups and had babies...
and *those* babies became grown-ups
and had babies...

Hundreds of summers and winters passed by...

...and the KEEP OUT curtain stayed in the temple.

Then, one day, God's Son came to live in this world as a person.
He was called JESUS.

Jesus always did what God said.
Jesus never sinned.

And Jesus visited the temple where the KEEP OUT curtain hung.

Jesus knew that things
were sometimes bad
and sometimes sad.

Jesus said that God had sent
him to open the way back
to God's wonderful place,
where there would be nothing
bad and no one sad!

But...

People still didn't want to
let God be in charge.
So they decided to put
Jesus on a cross to die.

It was the most bad thing that
had ever happened. It was the most
sad day of all time.

BUT...

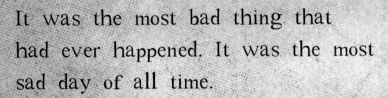

Jesus had a plan. He had always planned
to die on the cross. What a strange plan!
Why would God's Son plan to die?

On the cross, Jesus took our sin. All the bad things we do, and all the sad things they cause – Jesus took them all from us.

And when he did, something amazing, astonishing, astounding happened…

THE CURTAIN TORE!
God had ripped up the
KEEP OUT sign!

God's wonderful place
is open again!
Because Jesus died,
we can go in!

After Jesus died, his friends put him in a tomb.
They were very sad.

For two days, nothing happened.

Then, the next morning, Jesus' friends
went to see his body in the tomb...

AND IT
WASN'T THERE!

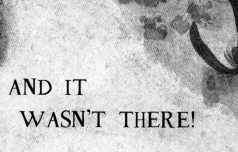

A little later on, Jesus' friends were all together...
and suddenly Jesus WAS there - alive!
  Suddenly, his friends weren't sad - now they were
so, so happy!

God had brought Jesus back to life
so that he could live in God's
wonderful place for ever!

And Jesus has sent everyone
an invitation to come and live
with him there too! He tells us,

God says it is wonderful to live with him.
Because of your sin, you can't come in.
    BUT I died on the cross to take your sin...

So all my friends CAN now come in!

We can live with God for ever!
There will be nothing bad,
and no one sad.

COME ON IN
FRIENDS!

We will see God and
speak to God and just
enjoy *being* with God —
just as he planned.

It will be wonderful
to live with him.
And it's all because
of JESUS.

We will say every day,

"Thank you Jesus!
You're amazing!"

And you can start saying

that... today!